Mentoring

Also by
Chungliang Al Huang
and Jerry Lynch

Thinking Body, Dancing Mind

Mentoring

The Tao of
Giving and
Receiving Wisdom

Chungliang Al Huang & Jerry Lynch

HarperSanFrancisco
An Imprint of HarperCollins*Publishers*

HarperCollins,® 🏛®, and HarperSanFrancisco™ are trademarks of HarperCollins Publishers Inc.

FIRST EDITION

Book design by Ralph Fowler. Set in Centaur. Brush calligraphic art by Chungliang Al Huang.

Library of Congress Cataloging-in-Publication Data
Huang, Al Chungliang.
Mentoring : the tao of giving and receiving wisdom / Chungliang Al Huang and Jerry Lynch. — 1st ed.
ISBN 0—06—251250—1 (cloth)
ISBN 0—06—251251—X (pbk.)
1. Interpersonal relationship. 2. Taoism.
I. Lynch, Jerry. II. Title.
HM132.H818   1995   95—2925
158'.2—dc20

95 96 97 98 99 ❖ RRD(H) 10 9 8 7 6 5 4 3 2 1

Contents

Authors' note: All interpretations of Chinese symbols and aphorisms are our best personal attempts to provide a creative translation of various ancient sources. We have taken the liberty of paraphrasing this sagely wisdom to suit the needs for our various offerings.

Tao Fa

Mentoring Along the
Watercourse Way

Those who seek mentoring, will rule the great expanse under heaven.
Those who boast that they are greater than others, will fall short.
Those who are willing to learn from others, become greater.
Those who are ego-involved, will be humbled and made small.

   Shu Ching

Although these insightful and prophetic words were spoken more than twenty-five centuries ago, the Chinese thoughts of wisdom from the ancient *Book of History, Shu Ching,* are perhaps even more relevant in our modern world with its deep and enthusiastic desire for self-expansion and personal growth.

   Today, there are many products and services available for self-actualization, learning, and personal growth, usually in the form of self-help books, magazines, computers, and other audio-visual technology, seminars, retreats, and so on. Yet a very important component is missing from these methods of self-growth: that of individualized, tailored, one-to-one environments for giving and receiving the gift of wisdom—the time-honored process of mentoring.

   The term *mentor* originated in classic Greek mythology when Mentor, a wise teacher, was asked by his friend Odysseus to watch over his precious son, Telemachus, as he embarked on a lengthy voyage. As a surrogate parent, Mentor gave support, love, guidance, protection, and blessing to the young child until the return of his father. Thus, we have come to know mentors as those who gently guide and nurture the growth of others during various stages of their development. However, the earliest model of the mentoring process was demonstrated in the succession procedures of the three Chinese sage kings Yao, Shun, and Yu, between 2333 and 2177 B.C. The passing of the throne by the sovereign to a virtuous and competent successor was known in early democratic Chinese history as Shan Jang. Literally, it means: "the enlightened stepping aside to create room in the center for the next deserving person to step in and take charge." Yao stepped out of the way for Shun, who in turn moved out of the center for Yu.

Over the years, however, mentoring as a means of sharing wisdom and learning seems to have become lost. Perhaps we fear appearing un-knowledgeable to others; it is simply too uncomfortable or even humil-iating to handle. For example, your boss asks if you have read a certain book, one usually familiar to people in your field and up-and-coming employees. Rather than look foolish or ignorant, you immediately re-spond, "Of course," and in the process you cut off an opportunity to learn. The Tao mentoring process makes such situations comfortable and safe enough to be open to "not knowing." In the corporate climate, a "Tao mentor" manager, rather than being critical or judgmental, is respectful and accepting of your honesty and sees this as a perfect op-portunity for you to learn something new and improve your skills and position in the company.

Tao mentoring is a two-way circular dance that provides opportu-nities for us to experience both giving and receiving without limita-tions and fears. If limits and fears are placed on either the giving or receiving of this gift, the process comes to a halt.

When your capacity for sharing wisdom is stunted,
so will be your fortune in receiving.

This mentor dance celebrates unusually gratifying unions of kin-dred spirits in soulful relationships. The Tao mentoring process is that particular crossroads in life where what you have to offer meets the immediate and future needs of another. Therein lies the enormous ex-ultation that is yours—that of giving your gift of wisdom and having it graciously appreciated and received by others who then carry the gift to all those within their sphere of influence.

Tao mentoring offers a new model of giving and receiving that in-corporates both ancient Taoist wisdom from the Chinese classics and new insights that we have gained from our experience as teachers, men-tors, and students. They are offered for anyone who wishes to cultivate healthy, harmonious, open-hearted relationships. Emperor Yao im-parts the following wisdom in the *Shu Ching.*

The Heart-Mind of the human is precarious,
The Heart-Mind of Tao is subtle,
One should be one-hearted and one-minded,
And hold fast to the Golden Mean.

This teaching reminds us to pursue self-cultivation through balance and harmony with the hope for dynamic and mutually satisfying relationships.

In the great spiritual tradition of Taoism, Tao mentoring contains the secrets of legendary warriors, kings, rulers, and other leaders—age-old principles of craft, skill, and indomitable spirit. These deep insights into human nature and personal conduct facilitate the process of teaching and learning, of giving and receiving wisdom in all relationships.

Every relationship is invited to enter this exciting journey of mentoring with the Tao along the Watercourse Way (Tao Fa, in Chinese), water being the ever present Chinese image of flowing transformation. According to the Tao, the best relationships are like water; they benefit all things and do not compete with them. Water is a natural element that ultimately changes the shape of whatever it touches; Tao mentoring changes the lives of the people it touches in a satisfying, positive way.

All relationships can be enriched by Tao mentoring: teacher and student, coach and athlete, manager and employee, therapist and client, husband and wife, parent and child, editor and author, clergy and layperson, and so on. It is equally relevant to the relationships between nations seeking to build partnerships. We have forgotten this ancient art, but if we introduce it into our relationships now, there is much good that can happen for ourselves and for the world.

The benefits of the Tao mentoring process, both personal and global, are numerous. The following is a conservative list of the payoffs of entering and following this process. You can expect to achieve:

The discovery of common ground between adversaries where nonviolent, win/win solutions can be created.

Support on your journey.

The ability to learn from failure and setbacks, nature's wonderful teachers.

A sense of loyalty and appreciation of others' journeys.

The ability to create safe, nonjudgmental learning environments where all points of view are truly heard.

The ability to enable others to realize and develop their full potential, by confronting and overcoming self-doubt and fear.

The ability to nurture harmony, cooperation, and unity of purpose among ourselves and globally.

Ways to ignite the flame of enthusiasm and passion for living that flickers in all of us.

A sense of acceptance, flexibility, and balance in your own life.

A spiritual rather than mechanistic view of relationships in all of life.

A strong sense of heightened self-esteem, confidence, direction, discipline, responsibility, and motivation on your chosen path.

A humanistic style of leadership, guidance, and teaching that benefits all within your circle of influence.

A clear, strong understanding of the interdependent nature of your relationships and of the interconnectedness of all life.

Let us now introduce you to *Jing Hwa:* The Golden Flower of Tao Mentoring.

Jing Hwa

The Golden Flower
of Tao Mentoring

Jing Hwa—The Golden Flower—symbolizes the quintessence of the Tao. Jing (gold) is the crystalline essence of the Taoist alchemy in the ultimate transformation and transcendence of the individual. The elemental eight petals of the Hwa (flower) represent the blossoming of the ultimate "thousand-petaled lotus"—the awakening of the real self, and the realization of wholeness in the human potential. Following are the eight building blocks, or cornerstones, of the Tao mentoring philosophy, which correspond with the elemental eight petals of Jing Hwa. They will assist you in emptying your mind of all the old ways of being in a relationship and opening it to new, refreshing attitudes and alternative healthy patterns in the giving and receiving of wisdom. Open yourself up to these eight philosophical petals of Tao and to your unlimited possibilities as you become initiated into the graceful dance of the Tao mentor.

Wu Ming
The Neutralization of Duality

More than likely, at this point you are asking yourself, "Who am I? Am I a mentor or a mentoree?" When given the choice, you may discover a strong gravitational pull toward one or the other. Western minds are trained to be dualistic; we are often most comfortable amid contrasts and distinctions. We are *either* beautiful or ugly; simple or complex; intelligent or stupid; liberal or conservative. The Tao, however, makes no distinctions. According to Tao, all existence is circular, a Yin-Yang process where black and white becomes richly gray: The Tao mentor is actually a superb mentoree; the excellent mentoree is a fine mentor. Both are akin to the Taoist ideal sage, an ever evolving Yin-Yang happy person.

The Chinese symbol of bamboo is a perfect metaphor of the Tao mentor, for it contains all the qualities of flexibility and strength, it is powerful and delicate, scholarly yet humble, with heart and mind in total balance. *Heartmind* is a combined word for the Chinese HSING, which means heart, mind, consciousness, and the life center. Bamboo's heartmind is the hollow-emptiness, the heartmind essence of the symbol for Chinese philosophical thinking. With Yin-Yang, there is no sharp line of demarcation; neither mentor nor mentoree can exist without the other. They define each other. Duality, therefore, within this Tao mentoring process is truly neutralized: The mentor and mentoree are much more than the sum of each individual part. This elusive concept, this paradoxical mystery where duality is neutralized into the confounding mystical area of no distinction, is called Wu Ming, the nondualistic Tao.

No longer can we tell whether it is the student offering himself to the teacher or the teacher offering herself to the student. We see each of the two beings mirroring the other in pure reflection.

 *Tui Shou*
The Dance of Pushing Hands

There is a classic Chinese story about two immortals who characterize the essence of the Tao mentoring relationship. Lu Dongbin had learned to become the ultimate good from his teacher, Han Zhongli. Yet, in spite of being immortal and all powerful, he was still in need of a mentor, just as the Jade Emperor, the highest god in his group of immortals, was still in need of Lao Tzu. One day Lu went to Han to ask how one learns the ultimate wisdom. Han replied that the true path to this wisdom is realizing "emptiness."

This is a crucial philosophical underpinning of Tao mentoring. One of the most powerful images that expresses the wisdom found in the "empty space" is that of Tui Shou, the Tai Ji (Tai Ji is the current, accurate spelling of the more familiar "Tai Chi" which is no longer used in China. The familiar "Chi" has been mispronounced over the years as "Ch'i," the other word for the Breath/Energy of life) dance of joining hands, an ancient yet timely technique for honoring the wisdom of joyful cooperation and synergy in human relationships. It is the dance between two willing and consenting partners, a dance of giving and receiving each other's gifts; a blending together in circular patterns as the hands surround the empty space between each of them. Just as the empty space or hole in a cup, glass, or vase defines its function, so too the space or emptiness that exists between two people during the constant dance of pushing hands in Tai Ji is the essence of the relationship, the wisdom in the empty space between both partners.

Clay is shaped into vessels, doors and windows are
carved from the walls, but the usefulness is in the empty
spaces. Benefit comes from what is provided, but
usefulness comes from what is absent.

This emptiness, a precondition for receptivity in the process of giving, is created by the natural movement of expansion (learning) and emptying (teaching) on the part of each individual in the Tao mentoring process.

Contrast the following difference between a Tao joining of hands in greeting and a typical Western handshake. In the West, handshaking rituals merely indicate surface contact between two people. Sometimes, handshaking seems to become a contest of "oversqueezing" each other's hands, an act of one-upmanship, a way of controlling an interaction. The only thing given and received is a reluctance to connect, which leads to the cutting off of potential intimacy. In China, although formality is appropriate during social intercourse, family members and loving friends often rely on lingering touch to perpetuate exchange and deeper understanding. The underpinning philosophy is that one must take time and open up to learning more about the other person. The well-studied Confucian maxim "Out of three in a company, someone would be my teacher" clearly indicates how aware the Chinese have been for centuries in recognizing the opportunities available when we share learning in our daily lives.

Wu Ji
The Empty Space of Wisdom

When two parties enter into the Tao mentoring dance, they create a safe environment where truth and wisdom can be discovered by both. Created is a sanctuary where the partners openly stimulate each other to discover the soul within. This "empty space," the fertile void of rich and everlasting resources, between giving and receiving is called Wu Ji, the place around which the Watercourse Way flows, the place of "not knowing," from which all is possible. With Wu Ji the mentoring process becomes limitless and free from the confinement of shape and form. Where Tai Ji is the great ultimate being, Wu Ji helps to create a relationship that goes even deeper, one that is totally liberated from constraint in the process of giving and receiving wisdom. Wu Ji is also the way of inner growth, which permits the water of life to flow into the gaps between partners' generations, countries, and leaders. This soft nonthreatening, uncritical, yet powerful flow enables partners to submit to not knowing, which, at times, may seem uncomfortable, threatening, or even painful. It is a passage rather than a path, to be experienced rather than achieved. Wu Ji gently gives permission for all of us, in all arenas of life, to face our vulnerabilities and insecurities in a light, humorous way as we flow to the vast empty sea of possibility and potentiality. Profound growth and change come when one is willing to let go and settle into the place of not knowing. To sustain this emptiness is to create enormous internal strength and wisdom, so we must take care not to rush in and fill it up. Learning to sustain it takes time.

*Do not assume that you know all. Notice nature and abide in
the infinite. Travel openly on uncharted paths. Be all that you are,
but do not make a show of it. Be contented and remain empty,
and learn to sustain the Beginner's Mind.*

Gu Shen
The Spirit of the Valley

Without this emptiness between mentor and mentoree, there is no
sharing. The emptiness enables us to learn enough—to get filled, as it
were—only to empty out once again in the learn-teach-learn cycle of
Tao. By mentoring others, we become aware of the gaps in our own
knowledge. Becoming dissatisfied, we realize that the problem lies
within, which causes us to feel stimulated to improve once again. This
dance of mentoring and learning stimulates self-expansion. When we
need to learn, we become open to receiving; once we have learned, we
immediately become open to giving. This is the never-ending process
of Tao mentoring.

This process is full of wonderful surprises. For example, one day
we (Chungliang and Jerry) were enjoying a session in which we began
gathering all of our research for this book. We've had a smooth, flowing dance since we first met, and this meeting was typical of our relationship. As we sat overlooking the beautiful winter surf in Pacific
Grove, California, I reflected on how Chungliang, born in China and
schooled in Eastern thought, worked so well with me (Jerry), an avid
student of Tao and formally trained in Western psychology. It seemed
that we pushed each other to go deeper into the understanding of
Chinese thought. Chungliang's encouraging, validating tone created an
ideal safe environment, the empty state of Wu Ji, which allowed me to
enter immediately with the open posture of not knowing.

Jerry's openness, interest, and enthusiasm for these ideas enabled me (Chungliang) to learn valuable new information; he also absorbed the dance movements that were happening between us in this process of giving and receiving wisdom. Upon returning home later that day, Jerry told me, he was visited by a close friend looking for help with a family crisis. Jerry was able to be a better mentor because he had been a good mentoree. He was ready to share compassion and love with his friend. The subject matter had changed, but the Tao mentoring process did not. He modeled exactly what had been practiced in our work together. For example, Jerry listened more attentively, and he made suggestions rather than try to control the direction his friend would take. He showed kindness and patience in an atmosphere of nonjudgment.

According to the *I Ching*, when anything reaches its extreme, it begins to change into its opposite. Sun leaves, moon comes; moon leaves, sun comes. This interplay of getting out of the way and making room for each other is the Taoist concept of Gu Shen, the Spirit of the Valley. The valley space, a precise metaphor for the Tao mentoring relationship, gives life, providing fertile ground by openly receiving the falling rain. As the fresh fallen water becomes a gushing river, trees and grass begin to grow, providing shade and food, nurturing the multitude of wildlife attracted to its pasture. The once empty valley now fills itself with life; because it is open, it accepts the warmth of the sun's strong nurturing rays.

 The Chinese written symbol for "mountain" shows three adjacent peaks with two valleys between, with Heaven above and Earth below. For Tao mentoring, we need to look at it all: peaks and valley, the full human. In Jungian terms, the valley is the soul (Yin), while the spirit is reflected in each peak (Yang). Having taken the time to understand the complexities within the valley, we become free to reach for the wide expanses of the peaks in all of life. It is this interdependence and multidimensional understanding of spirit and wisdom that is the philosophical essence of Gu Shen, the Spirit of the Valley.

The FIRE of the mighty river Yang
burns upward and outward.
The WATER of the quiet valley Yin
flows downward and inward.
And through their harmonious union,
the CHI begins to move and flourish.
And the Great Ultimate—TAI JI is born.

Wu Dao
The Dancing Wu Ji Mentors

All good mentors (giving, teaching) are continually open to being mentored (receiving, learning). To be a good teacher, one must be a good student. To be a good student, one must learn well what he or she will teach. Thus, the crux of the Tao mentoring process, as we see it, is the Wu Dao dance between mentor and mentoree, where each is involved with giving and receiving. The Tao describes this give and take, the constant adjustment of the mentoring Wu Dao dance:

It is likened to the stretching of a composite bow. The upper part is
depressed while the lower is raised. The extra (length) is shortened,
the insufficient (width) is expanded. It is the Universal Way to
take away from those that have too much, to balance with those that
have not enough. Only the person of Tao can do this!

In Chinese, the processes of giving and receiving are depicted by the elements of fire and water. Fire (or giving) is the life-force we feel from within the *dantien* (belly or reservoir), ready to be released outward and upward like a flame. Water (or receiving) is the Yin transformation of the Yang fire. It is soft and gentle, a rejuvenating quality that is received into the *dantien* at the completion of fire (giving), after our energy has been fully extended (when we have given).

To be a Tao mentor, one must be able to transmit, with compassion (and other Tao virtues) that which he or she has learned well as a mentoree. In Tao mentoring, each individual is interdependent in a relationship of mutual fulfillment, compassion, love, and respect, in an atmosphere of openness, communication, and loyalty. It is an egoless dance that encourages us to be empathic, to dig deep within ourselves for a selfless reflection of the other person's state of mind and reasons for action or inaction. We are one with our partner; we join and embrace each other in all the human dimensions; neither one is the guru because each has a wisdom that benefits the other. The only hierarchy, perhaps, comes from one or the other's concrete knowledge, but even this shifts back and forth. Teachers learn from their students what the students need to learn, just as parents receive from their children gifts of wisdom about many of life's emotional and spiritual concerns.

It is important to understand that this mentoring dance can trap us into feeling very noble. One gives the impression that he or she is so wise yet humble by "opening" to the "wisdom" of the mentoree, and when others notice it, they feel patronized. It's difficult to avoid becoming so noble in this dance and to genuinely experience the gifts each has to offer. Think, for a moment, of a teeter-totter: One instant you are up high; then, from that position of power, your body weight pushes you down, propelling your partner to the place of prominence. This constant exchange is mutually accepted.

Becoming a good mentoree is the first step in creating this dynamic, mutually satisfying relationship. Since the only thing that we ever really have to offer anyone as a mentor is the wisdom of our own experience, it seems crucial that we insist upon always being mentored ourselves.

In this never-ending Tao mentoring process, it is important to understand that one never actually becomes the wise one, the sage, so we are never burdened with that pressure. There's a scholarly teacher whose résumé reads like a "who's who" of American educators. Whenever he gives a lecture or seminar, he instructs those who introduce him to the audience to deemphasize his credentials to relieve him of the pressure of having to live up to such a billing. He is a Tao mentor. His low-key approach invites others to enter the talk, as they are not intimidated by his broad experience. He is willing to be a partner.

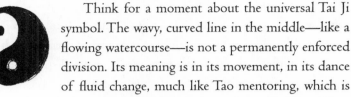 Think for a moment about the universal Tai Ji symbol. The wavy, curved line in the middle—like a flowing watercourse—is not a permanently enforced division. Its meaning is in its movement, in its dance of fluid change, much like Tao mentoring, which is neither too much Yin nor Yang; it is unity, it is dynamic change. True wisdom is the state when both giving and receiving are *intrinsic* to each member of the mentoring relationship.

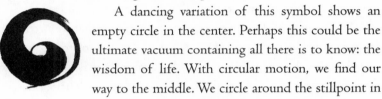 A dancing variation of this symbol shows an empty circle in the center. Perhaps this could be the ultimate vacuum containing all there is to know: the wisdom of life. With circular motion, we find our way to the middle. We circle around the stillpoint in the center and from there we can see the wisdom of all things.

Any person, at any age, can enter Wu Dao. The key to success with this mentoring dance is in the development of "Te" (as in *Tao Te Ching*). In Chinese, Te is the potential power of the individual who follows the Tao and his Heart, consolidating all his visions into spontaneous deeds and action. The symbol contains the Way (path) and the focusing of all senses (visions) into one Heartmind. Te requires the additional letting go of logic, of the need to pretend that we know all, and of the desire to display ourselves as sages. It asks us to admit that we "don't know," which creates a sense of wisdom that never relinquishes itself to fixed, limited opinions about what should be. By acknowledging this empti-ness, we enter into a communion with our partners, creating potential relationships of deep understanding and openness to vast growth and change.

Those who know they know not, become wise.
Those who presume they know much, stay ignorant.

When we are humble and modest, we command the respect of others; when we are empty, we are destined to be filled. Let's think about a Tao mentoring parent. Like all new mothers, she slips up and makes mistakes. During moments of weakness and failure with her child, her favorite "line" is: "Look, this is my first time—I'm new at this. I want to be the best mom I can but I'll need your help. When you goof up, I'll help you." If the child tells her what works and she continues to improve, the child becomes more open to listening to Mom when she corrects poor behavior. In the mentoring dance, all must be open to their emptiness, to not knowing, in order to learn and to teach. To put knowledge into perspective, recall the wisdom of Chuang Tzu, who reminds us that what we can know compared to what we cannot is but a squint compared to a full view of any situation.

The essence of Tao mentoring is in admitting that we need help on our path. The mentoree *asks permission* of the mentor to risk and to be vulnerable. If we fall down or make a mistake, it is fine simply to feel our insecurity and plunge back in, with the mentor's help. Now, go ahead and make a huge mistake, and trust that your mentor will help. Forge ahead, knowing that you are okay, able now to teach or mentor others who have fallen themselves. If we are afraid to admit that we "don't know," we may appear strong for a while, but the illusion will surface. And just think of all the energy it takes to uphold the illusion! Tao mentoring frees us to pursue life's wonderful lessons without fear of failing or being exposed.

Wu Wei
The Movement of Tao Mentoring

Wu Wei is effortless action, whereby you accept the natural way of life's events without imposing your will. When mentors and mentorees follow Wu Wei, they are in harmony with Tao mentoring. Wu Wei, the most subtle principle of Taoism, actually describes the lifestyle of one who follows the Tao, one who understands human nature and the complexities of life so well that he or she uses the least amount of energy and resistance when working with them.

There's a pertinent Wu Wei parable told by Chuang Tzu about a Taoist cook who follows the natural grain when cutting his meat, letting his sharp, thin blade seek its way easily through the hidden openings between bone and tendon. As a result, he maintains the sharpness of his knife, unlike the inexperienced cook who hacks away at the meat, dulling the edges and necessitating frequent changes of utensils. A more modern example is taken from the world of business, where failures and mistakes are natural components of the creative process. A good mentor-manager does not fight such a setback, nor does she force her employees to be perfect. The mentor knows that error is inevitable and encourages workers to accept failure and capitalize on the opportunity at hand: All mistakes are lessons that help us to improve. This effective Wu Wei manager removes the pressure to be perfect by rewarding those who find solutions to the setback. This approach creates unity and cooperation in an effortless manner. Wu Wei is a cooperative posture that transcends selfishness and goes beyond ego. Trust and sincerity are among its most powerful virtues. Wu Wei is the Watercourse Way, as one acts from the heart and follows nature's flow, just as when leaves fall, they follow the wind, land in water, and go with the flow.

One way to achieve Wu Wei in Tao mentoring is by what the Tao calls Jue Xue (acceptance of the idea that external knowledge is limited). This means that what we have learned is used not to impress others but rather as wisdom to help others benefit from our knowledge. Jue Xue asks not that you give up wisdom but that you avoid the pitfalls that accompany it—that is, flaunting it and becoming "wiser than thou."

Wu Wei movement comes with a certain level of experience; when we learn how smooth it feels to "blend" our efforts, Wu Wei becomes the obvious choice. Know that this takes time. Wu Wei, Wu Ji, and other Tao concepts come naturally with experience, wisdom, and maturity. When we get to know ourselves (as a mentoree), then we learn to respond to situations in life with great spontaneity (as a mentor).

Hao Jan Zi Ch'i
The Expansive Spirit

The Tao emphasizes the essential goodness in human nature. The primary goal in healthy Tao mentoring relationships is to affirm and nurture that goodness in both parties. The Chinese philosopher Mencius called this the "expansive spirit," or Hao Jan Zi Ch'i, which, metaphorically, enables us to enter and experience the air of the early dawn. When you rise early and go for a walk, you understand the essence of soft drops of dew and clean, pure air, cooled by the evening before and not yet contaminated by the exhaust from rush-hour vehicles. As you would love to protect and maintain the goodness of this air throughout the day, Tao mentors wish to guard the spirit or goodness of those they mentor. Therefore, the essential work of the mentor is to guide others to discovering this goodness within themselves and to help them follow their integrity as they reawaken to the inner truth of who they are and what they can do. For the mentor, this is a process of instilling mentorhood rather than embodying it. In Chinese, this inner strengthening process is represented by the ancient symbol of the Tai Ji mandala, the Great Ultimate, signifying all the powers of human nature. When given this power, people will accomplish the task, and when the work is done, they will say, "We have done it ourselves." For example, parents often make the mistake of forcing or coercing their kids into sports and other activities, thus causing resentment and counterforce in the children. Guarding and preserving the spirits and hearts of children is a delicate process. A Tao mentor parent listens to his or her children's passions and guides them softly in the direction they choose. In the process, the children truly discover their greatness within and believe that they did, indeed, do it themselves.

Similarly, there are many ways that the Tao mentor enables and nurtures the expansive spirit within the mentoree. The following examples illustrate the point.

A Tao mentor supports the dreams and goals of all within the relationship. "Thinking big" is always encouraged, as the mentor reminds others of what is possible in any area of interest.

The Tao mentor does not hesitate to give advice when asked. But most important, what is given is a blessing and permission to "fly" when one is ready. Naturally, close guidance rather than force is the key to this approach. For example, the mentor will notice in what direction the mentoree wishes to go and gently suggest ways to advance toward the goal. The mentoree then trusts that it's safe to move forward.

Mentoring provides valuable, timely feedback through candid conversation to create proper perspective. Principles of truth and honesty are strictly adhered to. A mentor in a professional relationship may tell an overenthusiastic, talented partner looking to advance that "it's not time yet" when the partner thinks he or she should be in the "inner circle."

A Tao mentor will enthusiastically tell others about a mentoree's talents, using her influence to give her partner exposure and visibility. Knowing that his mentor believes in him, his confidence level rises. In a healthy Tao mentoring relationship, the mentoree should not hesitate to encourage his mentor to speak on his behalf with regard to work opportunities or simply to make connections for future possibilities.

Through validation and affirmation, the Tao mentor promotes self-reliance, confidence, and self-realization in the mentoree. The mentor's faith in the mentoree helps to reduce fear and anxiety in times of chaos and crisis.

By creating a loving, compassionate, sacred environment, the Tao mentor enables mentorees to safely step out and risk failure, knowing that setbacks are simply lessons that help to guide the way. Often, the mentor will disclose how he or she struggled and failed in the beginning and how these setbacks were positive opportunities to learn and forge ahead.

A good Tao mentor can excite and encourage others through example, by displaying great passion and spirit. A certain flexibility, demonstrated by willingness to bend rules that impede progress, is a sure mark of the Tao mentor. In some cases, mentors might go as far as risking their own reputation in the face of adversity. A good mentor is not afraid to "stand up" for the mentoree who is caught between a rock and a hard place. Fighting for a partner—even when it's an unpopular stance—is often more important than going along with rules and regulations that make little sense.

When we engage in a Tao mentoring relationship, we can expect to feel free, alive, positive, energetic, and strong. We can expect to have our spirits—"the air of the early dawn"—preserved. The Tao mentoring relationship is the epitome of true liberation—physically, mentally, and emotionally. In such a dynamic, spiritual relationship, we will never stop growing and expanding as we are gently "pushed" into waters that we once feared.

> *A father asked his three-year-old son to come to the edge of the pool*
> *and jump. The boy said, "No, I'm scared." The father again encouraged*
> *him to come. The boy came to the edge but didn't jump. Again, the*
> *father gently asked him to jump. "I will protect you. . . . It's fun."*
> *And the boy jumped and screamed with incredible joy.*

Dao Ying
The Ideal Mentoring Relationship

Mentoring relationships usually come about when two people decide that the time is ripe for change, expansion, and openness to greater possibilities in all of life. Sometimes those partnerships are formed naturally, as between parent and child, professor and student, manager and employee, and so on. At other times, a search may be required, or perhaps circumstances may bring together two kindred souls. Regardless of how we come together, concern as to whether the relationship is an ideal one is common. After all, we have all heard about charlatans who use and manipulate people under the guise of being teachers.

What qualities do we look for when choreographing the dance of an important and ideal mentoring relationship? While there could be as many answers to this question as there are relationships, there are a few universal attributes to healthy mentoring relationships. Philosophically, the essence of an ideal mentoring process is close to the nature of the ancient Taoist concept Dao Ying. Here the symbol Ying shows the flowing path of Tao mentoring where the focused arrow, with bow fully expanded, centered and ready to be released, is confident and assured of the real "bull's eye," which is not *out there* but within the spirit center between the partners in this teaching-learning process. With Dao Ying, the mentor goes beyond the common notion of "master" to become a special kind of leader, one who can both guide and be guided. Dao Ying instills an attitude of trust that enables a mentor to say, "I trust that at this point you guide me. In the next moment I trust that you will respect my guidance of you." In this interdependent, unfixed relationship of mutual respect, each partner displays Dao Ying from moment to moment.

There are other attributes that define a healthy Tao mentoring relationship. For example, it is open, compassionate, and caring, and it exudes passion and inspiration for personal growth. Tao mentors walk side by side with their students to subtly guide and to open up options.

Tao mentors should be accessible and open to you, yet they are not necessarily your buddies. In time, you and your mentor may become friends, but do not assume at the outset that your mentor and you will have a close personal relationship. It's not a prerequisite for good mentoring.

Accountability in the relationship, however, is crucial. Does your mentor have a mentor? The best mentors are students of other mentors.

Humor is an important aspect of Dao Ying. Can your mentor laugh at his or her failures and mistakes, refusing to take him- or herself too seriously? Laughter is Tao.

Does he or she have an inner sanctum, a place to find sanctuary from the hustle and bustle of a busy life, a place to regain a common-sense perspective and energy?

Is your mentor willing to stand up for you when you're in a bind? Does he or she demonstrate a strong sense of commitment to the relationship? What kind of support is your partner willing to give?

Searching for a healthy mentoring relationship is not an easy task. Even though your need may be great, it could be a challenge to find a good one. The world is crowded with gurus seeking to fill their own needs for love, attention, even worship. Remember, the best situations instill you with self-love and respect. When looking for such a relationship, rely on your heart, your deep, intuitive sense of what seems right. Consider the above qualities and choose with care. If you are truly ready, the partner will probably appear.

To maintain Dao Ying in the mentoring relationship, we must move like wind and water in all of life. By going with the Watercourse Way, we can be as fresh as a mountain stream and as deep as the deepest ocean. Unlike the teacher who forces growth, the Tao mentor guides others the way sun and rain nurture the Earth—lightly.

Wang Tao

Cultivating the Virtues
of Tao Mentoring

When we enter into a Tao mentoring partnership, we begin a never-ending journey of self-transcendence and growth. This process helps us to cultivate an open heart-mind, enabling us to experience our interdependence with the world. The Tao considers self-cultivation and self-knowledge crucial to the process of offering gifts of wisdom to others. This level of self-growth is facilitated by the Tao Virtues of the Heart and the Soul. This path of heart and soul in Chinese is called Wang Tao, the Way (Tao) to develop the virtue of natural perfection (Wang). Virtue (Te) in Chinese depicts the power derived by following the Way of Nature (Tao) with all human senses—physical and spiritual—wide open, to concentrate on one vision with one heart-mind.

Tao gives life to all things.
Te fosters them, makes them grow, develops them
Gives them shelter—a place to dwell in peace
Nourishes them and protects them.

Tao gives life without possession
Te acts without claiming credit
Guides without imposition
This is the Mystic Virtue.

Effective mentors guide with virtue, without force or effort. In an atmosphere of inspiration, trust, courage, and harmony, where interdependence and personal strength are created, individuals begin to grow and become more aware, more conscious of their greater selves as well as the greatness in others.

What follows is a list of virtues derived from ancient sources of Taoist wisdom. These universal truths help those of us in the mentoring process to develop strong interpersonal bonds as we open deeply to the limitless possibilities within each of us. They are virtues that guide, rather than direct us on this journey of discovery and expansion. Discover for yourself their relevance in all arenas of life where teaching and learning are appropriate. By no means is this list exhaustive, and you will undoubtedly have a few entries to contribute as your thoughts are stimulated in this direction. Feel free to add as many as you feel are relevant, and use them appropriately.

The Tao sayings provide a comfortable space for meditation, contemplation, and imagination. The virtues presented in this section nurture the spirit of love, stoke the fires of the heart, and elevate the rich soul in each who engages in Tao mentoring, enabling the individual to become close kin to the Confucian ideal of Jen, or human-heartedness and benevolence. The Chinese symbol of Jen shows the virtuous relationship between two human beings as one of heart-filled compassion, love, and soulful regard for each other. These thoughts will help you to create safe, humane environments where you can give and receive wisdom in the spirit of emptiness (Wu Ji). They are meant for contemplation and to help us find our direction; they are not intended as doctrine. Notice how much is left unsaid, so that, like the emptiness, we can move in to fill the blanks, supplying personal meaning in each situation. These time-honored gems facilitate our transformation process, our path of discovering our greater selves—the very reason we enter a mentoring relationship.

The Tao virtues view people in a positive light, seeing all of us as capable of just about anything. It is time to recapture the essence of this vision. In Chinese, humaneness or humanized thinking actually means reasonable, truthful, virtuous thinking in accordance with human nature. Anything that departs from such human nature cannot be regarded as truth. To be unreasonable is to be self-righteous, while to be reasonable or humane is to entertain the possibility of not being right. Lin Yutang, in his classic work *The Importance of Living*, states: "The reasonable spirit humanizes all our thinking, and makes us less sure of our own correctness. It sounds out our ideas and tones down the angularities of our conduct." In this sense, humanism and Wu Ji are compatible partners for the Tao mentoring process.

We suggest that you read the following Tao mentoring Virtues (Te) of the Heart (Hsing) and the Soul (Ling) slowly and deliberately. Each virtue is presented in a four-page format. On the first page, you can experience the spirit of Tao by gazing at and meditating on the dynamic brush stroke calligraphy that depicts the virtue. Feel the power of this ancient wisdom through the art form. Take pleasure in the flowing movement of each character, along with what it depicts, and its special poetic meaning, which is provided on the second (facing) page. When you are ready to go further with the virtue, turn to the third page and enjoy our personal, creative translations of the epigramatic wisdom from various ancient Chinese classics as it relates to the virtue. On the fourth page, you will learn the practical applications of this wisdom and its relevance to modern times. When you reflect upon these thoughts, questions, and suggestions, take them deep inside and ask, "What does this mean to me? What are the implications of this wisdom in all my relationships and all of life?" See how you can apply the virtue in your present world. Discover how it resides deep in your spirit, your soul, your deep sense of who you really are and how you wish to be with others. We hope that, having read the four pages of each virtue, you experience the thinking-sensing-feeling-intuiting that accompanies it, thus creating an enhanced ability to receive and live this wisdom with clear, fresh insight. Take in the message easily, without effort or strain. Some of the virtues will feel just right and you will immediately apply them to your life. Others may seem distant. Let them be for now and move on, coming back to them at some future time. Remember that these virtues are truly beacons to illuminate the way. They are to be experienced, not achieved; they guide gently rather than direct forcefully.

Take your time to discover and enjoy Tao, the Watercourse Way, in all aspects of your mentoring relationships.

Virtues of the Heart

The cultivation of the Tao mentoring process begins with developing and nurturing the Virtues of the Heart. The Chinese describe "Virtue" with this popular saying: "Those who follow the Tao, with truth and fulfillment in their hearts, are indeed virtuous." Heart (Hsing) in Chinese implies mind/heart/consciousness. The symbol evokes the flowering center of the living force of nature and the unfolding of human nature as well. Mentoring requires us to open deeply to our pure and innocent nature, with all of our joys, sorrows, limitations, and possibilities. These Tao virtues require the courage to be soft and gentle, which, paradoxically, make us strong in our mentoring relationships. Ancient, universal qualities such as trust, kindness, patience, mindfulness, simplicity, humility, honesty, and others enable us to go beyond the hardnesses and blockages of the heart and strengthen the bond and connectedness of the mentoring relationship. By being true to the heart, we support and encourage our journey, our attempts to make sense out of what we do, and how we do it, in all our partnerships. When thinking about our most successful and worthwhile experiences in life, we find that they are the ones that were created in the spirit of love, with the voice of the heart.

Emptiness

The Chinese symbols depict
an empty space to be filled
and refilled as long as this
"fertile void" is maintained
in our deep awareness of
eternal renewal. When a
natural forest fire ignites,
a new clearing is revealed,
with the promise of the
new life.

In learning, we accumulate.
In Tao, we diminish.
To be empty we can be full yet
To be full we stay empty.
Abundance is within
Emptiness.

Most of us believe that teachers must know all. The wise Tao mentor knows that being aware of what is not known is important in order to begin to learn. Taoist sages claim that one who does not know actually knows, and one who knows really does not know. To attain true knowledge and wisdom, we must remain open and empty, allowing ideas from other people to rush in. To be empty, to recognize how little we know, is to be abundant. Consider the classic Zen story about a pompous professor who goes to the master to learn about Zen Buddhism. The Zen master invites him for tea, and to enlighten him, he pours the tea until the cup is overflowing. Then the master gently reminds him, "Exactly. Your knowledge is already spilling over, so how can I offer you any more?" How good it feels to be empty! But we must practice emptying our cup to be in a better position to receive. The Tao mentor actually strives to appear *less* knowledgeable than he or she is, and, in the process, commits fewer errors and mistakes. In this sense, real abundance is realized. This is the essence of emptiness, which is pregnant with potential and contains all possibilities. Emptiness is that humble Wu Ji place where anything can happen; the open cup into which the new "tea of learning" can be poured; the humble nothingness that contains all potential.

Humility

The Chinese symbols
illustrate an attitude of
deep respect in speech and
deed when communicating
with others, in sharing the
wisdom and knowledge
through learning, humbly.

With an attitude of unassuming modesty
you offer no danger or threat to those around you.
Sincere modesty
invites loyal alignment with others.
Do not boast and glare overtly.
Keep the jade and treasures
subtly reserved within the bosom.
A posture of humble heart and
genuine respect for the wise
will bring blessings from all directions.

Have you ever noticed that insecure people have a dire need to promote themselves? Those who brag without shame seem to experience great difficulty in living up to their image. Confucius tells this story about a warrior's display of humility: When his people were defeated in battle, he was the last to flee. So as not to look too boastful, he simply stated that his staying behind was due only to the slowness of his horse; as a result, honor and glory were his. We are more effective and appreciated when we are humble and focus on others' greatness. The Tao Virtue of Humility helps to ward off envy and unwarranted intimidation as it promotes easy heart-to-heart exchanges during the mentoring process, without any need to claim credit or to be responsible for full success in the end. So many of us feel the need to constantly prove our worth to ourselves and others. This is exceedingly harmful to our physical, mental, and spiritual well-being. Lin Yutang humorously describes the old Chinese etiquette of kowtowing to elders and superiors as the most sensible "whole-body" exercise for all ages, not only for the body but for the mind and spirit—bringing the stuck-up "heady-mental" self below the "gutsy-belly" self, a most organic way to keep fit and sustain humility. Taoist thought encourages us to be all that we have been given, yet act as if we have received nothing. In this way, no one will be aware of us yet we will bring happiness to all.

Self-Acceptance

The Chinese symbols describe a person with full awareness of self in body, mind, and spirit. This person's center of consciousness (Hsing—"Heart flower") is in full bloom, ready to receive power from above, openly relating to and being reflected by others.

It may seem clever to know and accept others
Yet accepting oneself is the way to Wisdom.
It may feel powerful to overcome others
Yet disciplining oneself is true strength.
It may be noble to honor others
Yet respecting oneself is deep self-esteem.

Notice how struggle enters our lives through self-doubt. It is not the inner fears and faults that matter; it is how we live in their presence. When we recognize our short-comings, acknowledge and accept them openly, true wisdom is ours, and we open up to the greatness within us. Return and return again to the secure and true self to a place of full awareness of body, mind, and spirit. Know that it is perfectly natural to have faults and doubts that may never be overcome or understood. Everyone does! Can we accept the whole self, with all its dimensions, and move on? Consider the tale of a man who hated his footprints: He ran faster and faster to get away from them, but the faster he ran, the more footprints he created, until finally he ran himself to death. Chuang Tzu shows us the value of uselessness with regard to self-acceptance by relating the story about the crippled child who, because of his infirmity, avoids conscription into war and obtains extra food and privileges out of regard for his condition. Many knotted and crooked trees reach old age, naturally perfect, because they are useless to the house builder.

Integrity

The Chinese symbols
illustrate wholeness and
refinement of character.
Together they denote a
commitment to stand up
for personal principles,
with constant mental
and spiritual cleansing
to keep oneself away
from tainted influences
and temptations.

Hold to your ethics and principles.

Stand strongly for what you hold true.

Believe in your true self without compromises.

Trust in the power within yourself and use it.

Act in concert with your dreams and visions.

Cleanse your heart and soul as nature renews itself.

Be honest with yourself and you will be aligned
with what is right,

in harmony with the natural laws of the universe.

What happens when we trust our sense about what's right, hold to our ethics and principles, and proceed to act on them in an honest fashion? Tao sages tell us that when we are true and honest to ourselves we hit upon what is right, find what is good, understand what's to be known, and create a life of harmony with the natural and moral laws.

Only by being true and honest to our inner selves can we fulfill our own nature and the nature of others and influence those in our world. When we are out of touch with our inner self, we feel fear. So we must maintain our integrity at all costs by identifying and cultivating our deep-rooted values. Only by knowing what they are can we act with integrity. We allow others to control our thoughts or beliefs and make us feel inferior when we act dishonestly about these values. What would happen if we acted from a place of deep self-truth to connect with the same deep truth in a partner? If being deeply honest threatens a partnership, should we continue it? Is it worthwhile? Integrity is the refusal to "sell out" on the true inner self, regardless of what situations in life present themselves; it is one of the most important aspects of the Tao mentoring process.

Kindness

The Chinese symbols
describe love and com-
passion in a friendly
exchange between two
human beings, mutu-
ally opening to the
larger part of our joint
human concerns and
understanding.

Loving kindness toward others will create
a spirit of unparalleled reciprocity.
Followers will become leaders,
leaders, willing followers,
jointly overcoming hardship
and honoring sacrifice toward mutual goals.
With loving kindness, you will win hearts.
Through compassion, you will gain loyalty
and cooperation.

The ancient story about the legendary kingdom of Shambhala serves as a model of peace and prosperity. The citizens were well taken care of by kind rulers, and in return they were kind, obedient, and giving to their rulers. It is said that the key to the success of this kingdom was the genuine love, compassion, and kindness exhibited by its leaders throughout its time. They gave kindness and received the same in return. The *Shu Ching* indicates that the length of a dynasty's governance is in exact proportion to the amount of love, compassion, and kindness showed by its rulers.

Loving, compassionate kindness in the Tao mentoring process creates mutual understanding and cooperative relationships. Confucius speaks of kindness as welcoming and protecting others; it commends what is good in them and forgives their ignorance. Notice what happens when people are cruel or harsh in your relationships. It is as if they've become hardened and lost their hearts. Mencius stated: "When people's dogs are lost, they go out and look for them, yet the people who have lost their hearts do not." Tao mentoring is a process of looking for and cultivating the heart that gets lost. We learn that we gain loyalty and cooperation when we are kind, loving, and compassionate. Then we inspire others, feel their spirit, and breathe life into their total being. Mutually, we overcome strife in the attainment of all goals and objectives.

Nonjudgment

The Chinese symbols
illustrate a fairness
of consciousness, by
regarding all under
Heaven as equal, and
a deep commitment
to balancing the dis-
crepancy.

Enlightened people do not judge.
Those who judge are not enlightened.
The way of Tao does not distinguish
and works without division and conflict.

The way of the Tao mentor is one of loving compassion, one that is beyond criticism or shaming. Judgment, criticism, belittling, and sarcasm are cancers that erode the mentoring bond and create unsafe environments, forcing the relationship to end. Notice that oftentimes what we criticize is something that we don't like in ourselves. For example, we complain about someone else being negative when, indeed, we are constantly seeing the dark side of things. Judging others, therefore, is often self-judgment. Does this attitude of judgmental intolerance separate us from or connect us with ourselves and others? When our thoughts and conversations are critical, how do we feel? How do we feel about those in our lives who have been judgmental, critical, or unloving?

Judgments are unnatural. If we follow the Tao, we naturally will be compassionate; compassion nurtures tolerance. When upset or angry with a partner, we must learn to be direct with our feelings without destroying the self-respect and esteem of the other person. Notice how strong we feel when we harmonize with nature and transcend judgment. Judgment is destructive; tolerance is constructive. Silence the critical mind and help it to dance with what is. At our deepest core, we are all innocent, pure, perfect spirits. We all have flaws and faults on the surface of our being. Honor them! Use them as seasonings while cooking a scrumptuous banquet in celebration of the divine human.

Trustfulness

The Chinese symbols evoke an inner sense of trust in others and in ourselves, the courage to follow the natural evolution of things, and the willingness to take responsibility as the person entrusted with this awareness and clarity.

Life's unfolding of events is as apparent
as the coming and going of the seasons,
the alternations of the sun and moon and the stars.
All things are exactly as they should be.

Trust is necessary when events and circumstances in our lives move and unfold contrary to how we think they should. If we trust nature, we will have no difficulty trusting ourselves. Without an underlying trust and confidence in nature, we become tense, stressed, and rarely meet with success. Tao mentors notice that all things are exactly as they should be; they trust the river's flow. Nature constantly sends us messages—omens that point the way, signs that help us follow our dreams. Progress may be slow, yet we must remain trustful of nature's way. What happens when we force or manipulate circumstances? Arrogance blocks the natural flow. When we plant flowers, we do not pull them up so they can grow taller and faster—we allow them to progress naturally. It is the same with mentoring. The following Chinese parable encourages us to trust what internally feels right, rather than trust some external indication of what may be right: A man was going to buy a new pair of shoes but forgot to bring the measurements, so he went home to get them. Upon returning he found the store closed, so he failed to get the shoes. Someone asked why he didn't just try the shoes on, and he replied, "I would rather trust the measurements than trust myself." Having personal trust is gratifying; do not abandon it even if things are temporarily unclear.

Inner Stillness

The Chinese symbols
represent the inner
peace attained by being
at ease with the gentle
and feminine Yin, the
receptive self, and the
calmness and clarity
that is attained with-
out striving.

Attain the utmost in emptiness.

Hold firm to inner stillness.

While all things grow and thrive,

Contemplate the turning cycles of life.

Flourishing as all nature is,

All returns to its source.

Returning to the Origin is to find inner quietude,

A return to claim our destiny.

This is constant and eternal.

To know this eternal constant is called Enlightenment.

Although for many of us, sufficient time for stillness is difficult to come by, we should realize that withdrawing, even for short durations, is beneficial, particularly during periods of frustration, crisis, or chaos. In the mentoring process, reflection enables us to slow down, rest, and observe our journey and the process of self-knowledge that is so important along the way. A person cannot see his or her own image in running water but sees it in water that is at rest. Only when one has realized growth and potential through inner stillness can one experience meaningful relationships and understand the universal laws of self-expansion. To help facilitate this process, the wise mentor takes the time to read and contemplate the natural rhythms and turning cycles of the partnership; how the relationship unfolds, grows, changes. Do we want to let life quickly pass us by, or do we want to turn inward and comprehend what transpires? To create outer movement in our lives, we must first find quietude. What would happen if we only viewed the world from the window of a train, or flowers from a galloping horse? We need to *stop, look* inside, and quietly *listen*—to what is truly happening. We all deserve sanctuary and time out along the way, a place where openness and wonder truly exist.

Mindfulness

The Chinese symbols
represent spiritual at-
tentiveness to the inner
voices of our deeper
selves, which reflect
outwardly to conform
with all our external
concerns.

Be in harmony with the Tao
which asks that you attend to small,
subtle details of things.
Be as mindful also when you interact
with all others in the world.
Your spirit will be whole.

Mindfulness, a state of relaxed consciousness, is the process of becoming aware of and acting in accordance with what we know to be right. It is the harmony created when we attend to subtle detail in relationships. Once we see, we act. As a practice of awareness, it requires being conscious of the implications of all of our actions, decisions, words, and movements. For example, mindfulness is the state of consciousness that warns us not to talk about our successes with one who is experiencing failure; and to remember our failures in moments of success. It requires sensitivity and the courage to perceive the world simply as it is at any given moment without judgment or criticism. Mindful Tao mentoring also encourages action—being attentive, caring, and seeing to it that others are treated with fairness. How do we feel when another is considerate and mindful of our needs and concerns? Can we learn to leave nothing to chance? Each day, we must notice ways to maintain mindfulness of our good fortune and the needs of others. There is no path to mindfulness; mindfulness *is* the path. It is the letting go of preconceived notions and of the tendencies to fix problems and to judge; it is a willingness to discover, explore, and appreciate what is with centered, trustful attention. When we do, our spirit will be whole.

似續

Attentiveness

The Chinese symbols
represent the virtue and
benefit of deep listening
by responding to others
"whole-heartedly" and
honoring the lessons
(treasures gleaned) to
allow meaningful trans-
formation.

Attentive listening to others is important

regardless of their stations and positions.

Wise people consider the deep meaning

and true values of all suggestions.

Learning and teaching are exchanged joyfully

through deep listening and mutual appreciation.

To create a safe environment and encourage open conversation, Tao mentors listen with full attentiveness, not with their ears but with their spirit, their full heart. When we listen quietly with our spirit and heart, we must be empty and ready to receive without judgment; we must tune in to the true needs of our partner and follow accordingly. What is right in one relationship may not be right for all relationships; listening attentively keeps the Tao mentor on track. When we "walk a mile in another's shoes," we develop a deep sense, through listening, of another's state of mind. When we truly listen and acknowledge another's feelings, problems are more easily solved. There is less fighting, criticism, fear, and misinterpretation; there is greater warmth, caring, cooperation, and a sense of clarity about important issues that affect the relationship. Learning and teaching are more easily and joyfully exchanged through deep attentiveness. Listen as well, to everyone regardless of society's biases of age or social status. How do we feel when we have something important to say and others refuse to listen . . . when they discount our contributions? Notice how easily communication, trust, and enthusiasm are extinguished in the absence of listening. Mentoring is a two-way communication system where either partner can be "right on" or "miss the mark." Keep an open spirit and heart . . . *listen* . . . in the safe, empathic environment of Tao mentoring.

Decisiveness

The Chinese symbols
suggest a decisiveness of
action with strong empha-
sis on clarity of thought
and wishes, and a determination to uphold the deci-
sion, as long as it comes
truly from the heart.

When the Mind is made up
according to the Heart,
And the Hsing is in accord
with Human Nature,
All your actions will be
in keeping with the Tao.
There will be no blame.

Tao mentoring adheres to the principle of decisiveness, a mindful state of assertive self-confidence in the relationship and a willingness not to destroy the process by being aggressive. Aggressive behaviors, whether physical or emotional, divide healthy alliances and produce a corresponding counteroffensive. Great teachers are able to be decisive and clear without the use of aggression. The *Shih Ching*, the Chinese book of odes, supports this notion: "All through the solemn rite not a word was spoken, and yet all strife was banished from their hearts." When one is intimidating, it suggests to others a deep level of insecurity and uncertainty about one's abilities. When Tao mentors are faced with conflict, they exhibit a "make no bones," self-confident, decisive determination with clarity of intent. The decisive route enables us to achieve our objectives more effectively. Taoists are true pacifists who understand the need to protect themselves and others from harsh interventions, and they do so, not by aggression but by exercising their power in a decisive fashion. When we are truly clear in the heart, we will find ways to proceed smoothly without obstructions. When we are decisive, we provide strong leadership and clarity in all relationships.

Perseverance

The Chinese symbols illustrate the strength, stead-
fastness, and unwavering
grounding in the spirit of
the individual. With heart
and compassion to embrace
and transcend inevitable
human sufferings, eventual
success and fulfillment
will be the rewards.

Great beings accomplish through perseverance.

Steadfast movement on consistent paths leads to success.

With heart full of compassion

Uninterrupted joy and good fortune are inevitable.

For those in a Tao mentoring relationship, it is important to have the ability to persevere during discouraging moments, in a deliberate, intentional manner. Confucius says that it matters not what we try to think or carry out; what matters is that once we begin we must never lose heart until the task is completed. Although we may make a thousand efforts, through steadfast and consistent movement we will surely attain success. To help persevere, focus on the joy of the journey, the process, rather than on the goal or destination. We need to be compassionate with ourselves when we seem not to be making progress. Regardless of whether we reach our goals, do we have the sense that the experience itself is worthwhile? Also, know that plateaus and setbacks are natural aspects of the Tao mentoring process. Embrace them as periods of deeper learning and mastery, rather than as unnecessary annoyances. If we ride out the difficult, discouraging times and follow the heart— what each person knows is right for him or her—we will eventually experience fulfillment. Let us not lose sight of what we desire or where we wish to be. With all its twists and turns, its changes of direction along the way, the river eventually finds its way to the sea. Endure with ease and hopeful anticipation.

Patience

The Chinese symbols
reveal a heart attending to
small details of human
nature and mutual needs,
as well as consideration
of others, with sensitivity
to adapt and adjust to
each other's wishes.

Observe calmly the natural unfolding of events.

Rapid growth and advancement are unnatural.

Hold to the inner vision of gradual flowering of potential.

Avoid haste. Do not jump ahead blindly.

Enjoy the moment of waiting to be!

Virtues of the Heart

While perseverance, a deliberate mind-set, keeps us constantly moving toward the attainment of a vision during times of discouragement, patience is the virtue that enables us to stay calmly focused and enjoy the wait as the vision unfolds. Lao Tzu encourages teachers and mentors to be patient. When we are, all will come to us. Rapid growth and advancement are unnatural, as we gradually open to our potential. Remember that things occur not when we think they should but when the time is right. Patience—the willingness to focus our energies and enjoy the process of waiting for things to unfold—helps us to live in harmony with the flow of life. Tao mentoring helps us to realize that we all need time and space to develop according to our natural process, to let our lives assume their own shape. Tao mentors are willing to repeat and re-create teaching methods and patiently allow time for ingestion and natural development. The Tao mentor savors the eventual moment when the sparks of the mentoree's apprehension ignite to illuminate their mutual learning.

Detachment

The Chinese symbols
instill a transcendent
spirit that breaks
boundaries and leaps
beyond self-imposed
limitations, to cast off
old skins and emerge
free from physical and
mental confinement.

Desires and attachments
to external circumstances
will detract and diminish
one's strength and personal power.
Suffering increases
as attachments linger.
Relinquish and transcend.
This is the way of the Tao.

Let us relinquish our attachment to outcomes; success or failure is not a barometer of self-worth. To be overjoyed at success and destroyed at failure is to become a victim of circumstances. Paradoxically, when we let go of attachment to goals and outcomes, achievement is often the result. Goals in life are simply beacons that illuminate our path, keeping us on the track of inner emotional and spiritual expansion. Is it more important to *achieve* than to find meaning in the *experience* of achieving? Notice how quickly we improve and develop when we focus on the experience itself and the process, the direction in which we're going, rather than on how quickly or "successfully" we arrive. Such focus reduces anxiety and tension over attaining a particular result, and the by-product is true achievement.

Tao sages encourage us to achieve perfect happiness through not being attached to happiness; perfect renown is the lack being attached to renown. Notice how freeing it feels when we detach from possessions, praise, and other ephemeral desires. Our greatest successes are usually the by-products of our most joyful processes. We will learn how effective we become when we open to the extraordinary power of detachment and desireless living.

Instinctiveness

The Chinese symbols
describe a direct entry
into the very center of
consciousness, with all
instinctual senses open
and focused to awaken
the wisdom of inner
knowing.

Pointing directly into the human heart
Seeing deeply into the true nature of being
You are instantly awakened!

Lao Tzu says that when we rely on natural insight, our inner sense, life will be free of misfortune. Tao mentors know that human instinct is real knowledge, based on insight and the wisdom from our true nature. They encourage instinctive responses that inspire and gain the trust of others. When we act directly from the heart in a relaxed, spontaneous manner, we become more effective, influential, and aware. As a result, we better understand situations as they develop and react quickly and decisively. When we reflect deeply into our true nature and upon our past experiences, the times that really stand out as successes are usually the times when we trusted and acted according to the wisdom of the heart—our instinct—and that's the best part. Why do people continue to search for data to justify their actions when all the information they need is available through trusting their instincts? The Tao asks that we develop a feeling about life's patterns and movements by opening and focusing all of our senses and awakening to our inner wisdom. Avoid overanalyzing and excessive thought. Human instinct is natural; when we align with nature's way, we gain direct access into the deepest part of the self and stimulate the wisdom of true knowledge.

Simplicity

The Chinese symbols
teach an awareness of the
simplicity of being. They
represent unadorned na-
ture with the essence of
being in the woods or en-
tering the bamboo gate
into the open clearing of
a typical Chinese court-
yard to enjoy the sun-/
moonlight from the sky.

Tao is naturally without a definition.
Although it is small,
nothing can surpass its primal simplicity.
When leaders abide in Tao,
everything will harmonize.
Heaven and Earth will unite,
and sweet rain will fall.
Peace will reign among the people
without command from above.

The Tao mentoring process encourages us to follow one of nature's most subtle and paradoxical laws: Less is more. This is the "Great Way." Lao Tzu states that "if I had any wisdom, I would choose to walk the Great Way." The Way (Tao) is very simple, but people prefer to confuse themselves with devious paths.

Ancient Tao mentors did not overwhelm others with enlightenment and cleverness, but rather kept themselves in a state of simplicity. This is called the Mystical Virtue. Deep and far-reaching is this virtue, for it turns all things around until they come back to arrive at the Great Harmony.

By following the Great Way we truly simplify the journey and create a sense of inner freedom. Keeping the mentoring relationship uncomplicated—communicating your feelings honestly and directly, listening attentively —strengthens the partnership and contributes to its overall harmony. Try interfering less and instead trust the flow. The temptation to offer more when the simple ways are not immediately working only complicates and confuses matters further. Recognize how happy you are when things are not so complex, when life begins to present moments of pure simplicity. Unburden yourself of complexity; become more plain and simple.

Virtues of the Soul

Whereas the Tao Virtues of the Heart strengthen the personal bond between two kindred spirits in the Tao mentoring relationship, the Virtues of the Soul inspire us to attend to the intricate details and mundane realities on the path of the mentor. Virtues of the Soul prepare us to confront the conflicts, doubts, failures, paradoxes, and adversities of life while giving us the strength to develop the self in the process. They inspire us to choreograph a special multidimensional relationship with deep soulful substance. Soul (Ling) in Chinese implies a connection of the Spirit with Heaven (ascending) and with Earth (descending) through the phenomena of powers from the sky and the earth, and the magic of the shamanic healing arts. Subtle soul virtues such as empathy, spontaneity, nurturance, guidance, centered heart, and others are transcendent, taking us to places deep inside and enabling us to be more sensitive to the needs of a partner as we travel together to greater spiritual and emotional depths. The Virtues of the Soul create dynamic, satisfying situations by gently guiding us, in spite of our fears, to feel and reveal the innermost aspects of self, giving us a clearer sense about our relationships with others from the inside out.

Service

The Chinese symbols suggest a mutual sharing of human needs, and active support, both physical and spiritual, to serve the greatest interest in one's relationship with a partner.

Generously offering oneself
in service to others
inspires loyalty and a freedom to ask
for advice and guidance.

The Tao mentor knows that to mentor truly is to serve.
When leading, teaching, or governing, the leader is least
important, the people are the most important. The
teacher who offers herself in the service of her students
becomes richer. Giving *is* receiving and when we serve
with honor, our partner gives back one hundredfold.
In sports, such as tennis, to "serve" a ball has deep
metaphoric meanings—it is an offer to begin the game
(the mentoring dance) and a readiness to receive the
return of the "serve." When we instill in others their
own greatness, we, in turn, will be great. When we truly
serve others, we experience loyalty in an environment
of mutual benefit.

A Chinese parable describes the settings of Heaven
and Hell exactly alike: Each is an enormous banquet
with delectable dishes on huge round tables. All are given
chopsticks five feet long. In the banquet in Hell, people
struggle to manipulate these awkward utensils, give up
out of frustration, and starve. In Heaven, everyone serves
the person across the table and each becomes abundantly
full. Those who follow the Tao attain great fulfillment
through loving service.

Modeling

The Chinese symbols separately
illustrate a scholarly and poetic
matching of verses through mutual inspiration. This is comp-
arable to the joy experienced by
kindred spirits as they create
their interchangeable and recip-
rocal couplets in rhyme. These
characters also encourage us to
follow in the tracks created by the
wheels of a leading guiding vehi-
cle, much like the respect given to
those who paved the way before
us, our lineage and ancestry who
are our teachers and sages on this
path through life.

The Sage embraces the One
and becomes the Model for all.
Does not make a show, hence shines.
Does not justify, hence manifests virtues.
Does not boast, hence deserves praise.
Is not ostentatious, hence is followed.

Virtues of the Soul

Model for others what you want others to model for you. This is the Golden Rule. If you relate to others exactly as you wish them to relate to you, both of you will be grateful. The wise mentor does not impart feelings, attitudes, and knowledge in an ostentatious manner; through modeling and demonstration he or she influences the surroundings, and by so doing receives praise and the loyalty of others. It should be noted, however, that not all paths modeled by mentors will be appropriate for you. Do not follow or imitate blindly. We must have the courage and the creative incentive to venture into the unknown, and humbly expose our inevitable faults. Ultimately, our personal passion will be honored if we are acting out of the deepest core of the true self.

This concept of teaching by modeling and learning by imitation mirrors the Confucian ideal of the "superior person." By modeling virtuous behavior, we have an enormous impact upon others. Follow the way of bamboo, which models growth through resilience and the upward action of its shoots.

Guidance

The Chinese symbols
show an open gate with
two brilliant lanterns
pointing to the source
(the wellspring of all possibilities), and leading the
way to the spring, step
by step, with wisdom
and care.

Tao guides with the Watercourse Way.
Uses little intervention, no manipulation,
no imposed morality, no coercion.
Shed light to show the way.
Suggest the choices, and let
them feel a personal initiative,
and say, "We did it ourselves!"

The Tao mentor gently and subtly guides, rather than controls, others. Wise leaders encourage others to be more self-reliant and discover what is best for themselves. The exertion of control over a situation or person is emotionally expensive for all involved and exhausting to the one in control. It blocks visions and all creative possibilities. Controlling behaviors create a sea of mistrust, lack of cooperation, and loss of faith in the mentoring process. The Chinese symbol for control honors the way of letting be, allowing natural forces to prevail through guidance. Notice how much more powerful we feel when we choose to step subtly out of the way and simply guide others without imposing our agendas. Only when we dare to let go of control will we win the hearts of others and enable true learning and growth to occur. Let others find their own way by using very little intervention; refrain from manipulating, imposing morality, or coercing. Shed light through suggestion. Confucius, in his discourse on education, states that the "superior teacher [mentor] guides students but does not pull them along; urges them to go forward by opening the way yet refrains from taking them to the place." Guiding creates an atmosphere that encourages others to think and accomplish for themselves. The Buddha says that the best way to control your cow is to not control it. Offer, instead, a large, spacious meadow.

Empathy

The Chinese symbols
illustrate a natural sensitivity to the feelings of
others and how to re-
spond to their needs ac-
cordingly, in a deep,
heartfelt way.

To feel and resonate deeply in your heart
the thoughts and wishes of others,
To care and respond with love and kinship
With hearts open — a joyful song is harmonized.

One of the most overlooked capacities of human nature is that of empathy. This virtue conveys how deeply and sincerely we feel *with* another in the relationship. It is that rare quality of being able to "walk a mile in another's shoes" and live, for that moment, their experience and life as it appears to them. To be empathic is to fully understand one's partner and to communicate through words and action that you are in tune with them. We often fail in daily communications because we assume too much and take little time to feel and sense others. The Virtue of Empathy is indeed crucial in Tao mentoring, for this is where we take the time to reflect the feelings and responses of another. We are reminded of the metaphor from the *I Ching* of "Wind over Water," which suggests the rippling waves reflecting all the moods of the skies. We must learn to touch our partner not only with our words and physical actions but with our deep thoughts and senses as we invite the other to experience the love that resonates within the partnership. Trust this gift of mutual empathic awareness and sensitivity, and rejoice in the music of each other's unique voices harmonizing together. The "Inner Truth" hexagram of the *I Ching* has this verse:

> *A crane sings in the shade.*
> *Its young harmonize.*
> *I have a good wine*
> *and fine goblets*
> *to share a toast!*

Nurturance

The Chinese symbols
illustrate the process
of rainwater making all
nature grow, and the in-
stinctual behaviors of
all species to nurture
their young.

Care for all seeds ready to sprout.

Encourage all shoots to reach the sky.

Offer inspiration to grow and flower.

Feed the hunger of the Heart and Soul.

When cultivating a young rose bush, we foster the new life in fertile soil, give it plenty of water and sunshine, and prune it appropriately, thereby encouraging rapid, healthy growth. From a simple seed comes a beautiful fragrant flower because we took the time and effort to nurture it throughout its growth process. Tao mentors know it is no different with those whom they mentor. They affirm, inspire, and nurture greatness within others in an environment of hope and inspiration—a place where the soil is fertile for healthy growth and change.

The instinct to nurture is most obvious in parenting. All parents can bring to the mentoring process this instinctual love and affection that we express toward our children especially during moments of insecurity. Parents/mentors are greatly rewarded when the same kind of caring and affection is reciprocated from their children/mentorees. It is an act of true giving and receiving, serving one another the Food of the Souls.

In Tao mentoring, nurturance also implies the instilling of courage, giving us permission to follow the heart, our passion, in all that we do amid life's tests of patience and trust. Nurturance helps us to see how nature conspires to provide what we need along the way; doors seem to open to us when we truly follow the heart's desire.

Harmony

The Chinese symbols help us to visualize a leveling of opposites, a meeting of east and west, and a vision of the horizontally suspended ease and freedom of "fishes in water."

Act with the focused strength of the Masculine
And keep the nourishing softness of the Feminine.
Embrace the magical harmonious dance of these opposites.
Enjoy this dynamic fusion in your being.

The wise Tao mentor pays attention to creating harmony between the two poles of cosmic energy, the magical dance of opposites, Yin and Yang. Yin and Yang are inextricable internal entities, natural components of one's total being. They represent a symmetrical interplay of the natural forces, such as night and day alternating, warm and cold seasons changing in cycles, and woman and man coupling in harmony. The Tao mentoring process is based on transforming duality into Yin-Yang balance. Tao mentors are rational, decisive, and powerful, as well as intuitive, healing, receptive, and nurturing. The mentor dance is a perfectly harmonious union between two people, one of perpetual interaction and fluid change. In this Yin-Yang dance, neither is rigidly fixed. Trying to be more of one to the exclusion of the others creates disharmony. By itself, the rigid, unyielding Yang falls to the wind, finding its weakness, paradoxically, in too much strength. Visualize the dynamic balancing act of an exciting tennis or Ping Pong match between two players of equal skill. This is the best example of a possible win-win game in which both parties are in blessed, harmonious accord.

Cooperation

The Chinese symbols
represent a oneness of
vision, with many joint
efforts, sharing one
heart and one reason.

Heaven and Earth join spontaneously
To create soft rains and gentle flowers.
Sun and Moon move alternately
To shed lights of Yang and Yin.
Man and Woman love naturally
To propagate and nurture life.

Cooperation is part of being human. The human spirit is enhanced and strengthened through the efforts of working together. The Tao mentor realizes this and therefore promotes cooperation in relationships. Ancient cultures strove for spiritual togetherness and the cooperative reuniting of the hearts of their people. Today, families join together to help those in need, whether to raise a barn or to perform other tasks within their communities. Large corporations are now, more than ever, recognizing the benefits of team building.

The key to triumph in all of life is unity of purpose and mind. When we lack cooperation, we create alienation, which obstructs life's flow. Tao mentoring requires healthy collaboration and teamwork. Think about the last time you experienced a cooperative association and how it affected your life. Notice how the relationships that exist for each other exist eternally. The wisdom of Tao reminds us of how Heaven and Earth, through cooperation, create soft rains and gentle, sweet-smelling flowers.

Interdependence

The Chinese symbols de-
scribe a joining of polar
opposites to form an open
center, and the mutual in-
forming of the natural
process of the Yin-Yang
transformation in the
eternal quest of Tai Ji
wholeness.

The most healthy and enlightening relationship
between two people is one of mutual fulfillment,
as in the Yin-Yang polarity when interests are aligned
and individuals share a common goal,
and a joint process in the Dance.

Tao mentors know that everything in life is interdependent. Every event or person is what it is only in relation to all others. The Chinese principle of Hsiang Sheng ("mutual arising") proclaims that all things are mutually interdependent, and if allowed to go their own way, harmony in the universe will result. How good it feels to know that we can depend on our mentors and be dependable for them. The Tao Virtue of Interdependence helps create stronger mutual support when needed. This is not to be confused with codependency or unnatural clingings. At its best, interdependence allows us to experience the euphoria of our interconnectedness with all things and all beings in life, recognizing the true magic of this Taoist wisdom of mutual arising, as well as the most blissful personal well-being.

In the Tao mentoring process, both partners need to be present for each other and recognize their mutual contributions. There can be no Yang without Yin. Contemplate how the ecosystem works in oceans and forests, and in natural phenomena such as the works of earthworms, ants, and pollinating bees. Everything has its purpose in the universe. We see the intricate interconnection in our relationships at work and in the family, and the way in which the people and patterns of our lives are intimately related to one another, how everything is connected within the greater whole.

Yielding

The Chinese symbols
illustrate the way rivers
and streams mold and
form their paths according
to the dictates of the natural contours of the land;
and suggest for humans,
to go along and enjoy the
mountain curves and the
Watercourse Way.

It is wise to swim downstream
and more scenic
curving around the mountain.
Adapt to changes
and enjoy the new circumstances.
Yielding rises with pleasure as
Resistance falls in disgrace.

Sometimes, life's events and circumstances are contrary to our immediate plans and wishes. Resistance to unpredictable change is pointless. The wise Tao mentor demonstrates leadership and strength by spontaneously creating new behavior patterns that are flexible enough to yield to sudden changes in life. Mentoring relationships that are yielding expand, rise, and create pleasure; those that are unyielding atrophy, suffocate, and fall in disgrace. When surprises spring upon us without warning, consider how the Chinese love the yielding qualities of bamboo and willow trees; because of their great strength, they bend and move easily during heavy snow and turbulent windstorms. When nature bends and yields, it creates great beauty in graceful curving patterns that we admire. There is wisdom in following the naturally curved paths in life rather than the most efficient, straight-line roads. Avoiding the four-lane speedways often creates the most meaningful experiences of living as we yield along the "roads less traveled." Happiness and peace are ours when we adapt to changes when they appear. Chuang Tzu tells the story of a drunken man who falls off a cart without injury, because he yields to the fall, and is completely at ease with his new predicament. The body without tension and the mind without intention are most adaptable to changes that deal with life's many demands and unpredictable circumstances. Yielding conquers the resistant; soft triumphs over the hard.

Enthusiasm for Change

The Chinese symbols show
us the metamorphosis of
a chrysalis and the coming
through of the inevitable
transformation; and after
all obstacles are cleared,
everything flows naturally
once again.

Notice the changing cycles of life.
Welcome and respect these changes.
When the changes of the Universe
have run through their courses,
transformations ensue.
Through decline and decay,
they move on and circulate.
By continuing to recycle,
they attain eternal life.

Never confuse change with chaos. The Tao mentor
knows that nature is constantly in motion, changing pre-
dictably according to predetermined laws. Seasons are
cyclical; moods shift—some days we're up, others we're
down; we're well, then ill; hot, then not. According to
the Tao, nothing is static. Tao is without beginning and
without end; each end is a new beginning. The mytho-
logical phoenix descends into ashes and quickly rises up,
expressing the exuberance of a new life. The wise mentor
notices with enthusiasm the cycles of change, respects
them by refusing to interfere, welcomes them and encourages us to dance enthusiastically with the pulses and
rhythms of such transformations. Recognize constant
change as a teacher, and take the unpredictable variations
as challenging opportunities to develop new patterns of
behavior and a strong inner sense of self. What happens
to us internally when we show a lack of enthusiasm for
these cycles of change? Life is a moving pendulum, a
back-and-forth process that never ends, constantly re-
cycling itself as it gains eternal life. If you don't like a
situation, know that, in time, it will change.

Joyful Laughter

The Chinese symbols picture a laughing human with arms wide open, legs kicking outward, face up to the sky, laughing like bamboo leaves in the wind; and the joy of music making, with the invigorating sound of bells, gongs, and drums resonating and harmonizing.

The Happy Buddha awakens all
with joyful laughter, rhythm and dance.
The Chi of life enters
the palms of hands and the soles of feet.
The body enlightens while
The soul soars.

The Tao is often called the Way of Laughter. Tao mentoring cultivates the natural universal sense of joyful laughter, the importance of which cannot be overstated. Notice the effect of good wit upon others as it softens the sharp edges of our thoughts and experiences. The inability to see the humor in life's absurdities or to laugh at one's failures is costly. Confucius always took criticism lightly. He was once told that he looked like an emperor yet crestfallen like a homeless wandering dog. He didn't think he resembled an emperor, but he admitted to resembling a homeless wandering dog. Think about what happens to us when we take life and ourselves too seriously.

We know that hearty, joyful laughter actually stimulates the release of endorphins, the body's natural anesthesia. Laughter alleviates pain; it truly is the best medicine for a myriad of emotional, spiritual, and physical dis-eases, all of which improve with good humor. Notice how humorous thinking promotes well-being and harmony in partnerships, enabling the mentoring process to thrive in a spirit of happy play. Laughter restores one's perspective. When you get stuck in your thinking, try laughing with gusto.

Spontaneity

The Chinese symbols
represent the embodi-
ment of nature in one-
self, and pictorially,
illustrate a primal scene
of a wolf howling at the
moon by a bonfire.

The Wind and Water follow
the paths of their own flow.
They in turn shape and form
the Beauty we call Nature.
Windflow (Feng Liu) is
the Grace we all admire
and wish to embody.

Being spontaneous is a gift of creative improvisation, when we act most appropriately and in a timely way. To be present in the *here and now*, and to be naturally so, is a virtue to be cultivated and admired.

Avoid the pitfalls of presumptions and anticipations, which often disappoint and misguide. To honor our own true nature is to open doors for others to understand us better. Individual style develops easily according to one's own way of acting naturally. Often, seemingly weak, idiosyncratic traits turn into admirable character strengths when we honor our own spontaneity and simply let ourselves be. We must not pretend to be other than who we are. Perfect who you are and notice the perfection in others. Encourage and appreciate others' spontaneity, and reciprocate with trust of these genuine expressions. Let us challenge ourselves with the opportunities of improvisation, and enjoy the natural developments of this immediacy and alertness in our relationships. Great things happen as they are supposed to in spite of our desire to control them according to our wishes. Yes, each of us can smile and say, "How wonderful, it just sort of happened!"

Vigilance

The Chinese symbols
teach us to respect wis-
dom, to look ahead for
advanced signals, and
to be willing to have a
change of heart accord-
ing to the shift and
change of circum-
stances.

Entertain hardships while they are still easy.

Address great issues while they are small.

The wise take precaution, and anticipate

difficulties with ease and preparation.

And manage to accomplish great things.

All major problems in relationships and life in general can be prevented by being conscious and vigilant of problematic patterns in nature. Making proper precautionary decisions can ward off major crises, disease, starvation, and many forms of environmental and personal pollution. Preventing problems requires us to anticipate their possible occurrence by the practice of vigilance and cautious alertness. We must learn to anticipate with preparedness, knowing what to expect and to be ready for action. Notice how easy life becomes when we anticipate and intervene while problems are small and easy. Tao mentoring relationships thrive when partners are alert to potential difficulties and take the proper measures to prevent their occurrence. Mentors need to be like meteorologists, posting small-craft warnings, travelers' advisories, and other signs of an impending natural disaster prior to its occurrence. Knowing that a hurricane is in the forecast, we may want to board up the windows and fill the cupboard. We must be vigilant of adverse emotional "weather patterns" in our relationships and take correct measures to soften their impact.

The wisdom of Tao tells us to tackle problems before they appear; practice peace and harmony, and we will be prepared to deal with confusion and chaos when they arise.

Centered Heart

The Chinese symbols
depict a centered body-
mind-spirit disposition,
properly collected and
balanced within, with
a fully expressive and
blossoming heart.

When the position of the body is correct,

and the heart and mind are in the proper place,

All things will come together to affirm and celebrate life.

And the world will be rejoicing in peace and harmony.

In the process of growth and learning, mistakes, set-backs, and failures are inevitable. When a centered, open heart and mind come together, the Tao mentor is able to see these occurrences simply as nature's lessons from which to learn and go beyond. This Heart-Mind Unity is the Chinese symbol of Hsing and affirms the way nature always focuses her consciousness in the "stamen of the flower." Centered focus gives us positive observation and tenacity to all of life's ups and downs. With the Virtue of Centered Heart, our failures will ultimately be our triumphs. Focus on the rewards in failure as in success, and as a result attain peace and joy in the process. When we embrace a setback we learn from it and progress accordingly. To fail to learn from this opportunity is to commit another mistake. Remember that the arrow that eventually hits the bull's-eye is usually the result of a hundred corrected errors. When we think back on the major defeats, mistakes, or setbacks in life, we see that an opportunity came from the adversity. What was learned? The word for *crisis* in Chinese contains two distinct meanings at the same time: danger and opportunity. Remember that the dawn always follows the darkest moment of the night. Times of progression usually are preceded by error and setback. You can learn and grow from any failure with Centered Heart.

Consistency

The Chinese symbols illustrate the enduring mix of
light-and-dark of the sun-
and-moon alternation, and
show the treasure in the
constancy and reliability
of the "Mother Earth."

Consistency ensures self-reliance and inspires self-direction.

Guide and direct others with love and oneness.

Follow nature's course with full-heartedness.

Trust one another like mother and child

and know that sun and moon shine eternally.

Realize that inconsistent, unpredictable behavior patterns within relationships are unsettling and erode the confidence and trust so necessary for a productive and fruitful partnership. Do we want to create peace and stability, or would we rather contribute to chaos? Notice how effective and influential we become when our actions are consistent and comfortably familiar. Ask yourself: How would I feel in an environment where I always had to walk on eggs, one of inconsistency and unpredictableness? Tao mentors create love, order, safety, and comfort when they are consistent; disorder and chaos when they are not. Realize that while so much inconsistent behavior is going on outside ourselves, we simply need to get in touch with the voice of the heart and transmit what works for us to others in our environment. We must be consistent in our approaches and ways of being, and avoid erratic behavior that would create insecurity, tension, and fear. Be accountable and dependable with the variations of the "patterns of life," and be clear with the core intentions to instill trust and mutual ease and comfort.

Moderation

The Chinese symbols point
to the middle to prevent excess. They illustrate an inner
strength and awareness to
remain uncluttered from the
burdens of unwarranted
desires.

Excessive craving for things will cost dearly in the end.

Hoarding too much will bring a heavy loss.

To be content is to be free from disgrace.

To stop in time is to be preserved from danger.

Tao mentors teach moderation in the process of seeking our highest good. Extremes of up and down are interrelated. Excessiveness ushers in disorder and disaster, which lead to burnout and fatigue as we walk the way of personal destruction. The path of any spiritual practice or philosophical change requires us to be nonexcessive lest we fail to adjust properly and thus render all meaningless. In leading others, there is nothing better than moderation. To have enough is good luck; to have more than enough is harmful. This is true of all in life. Leisure is good, yet too much can lead to restlessness and boredom. Work is important and beneficial, yet in abundance it can cause havoc in other aspects of life. Learn to enjoy periods of aloneness in which meditation contributes to clarity, as well as times of social gregariousness in order to exchange affirmation, love, and togetherness. Exercise ushers in a vibrance and wellness that makes for a healthy, happier life, yet, in excess it can strip us of the vitality accrued. Moderation allows us to dance between any two extremes with great agility. What in life works well in excess? Notice the varied possibilities and personal satisfaction we experience when our lives are devoid of extremes. Learn to walk the Moderate Way, the wisdom of centered contentment. Avoid the temptations of overdoing and overextending, no matter how enticing and attractive the pulls and lures might be.

Tashun

Humble Visions for a
Harmonious World

When we observe the world with all of its multidimensional relationships, we cannot help but notice the abundance of strain, struggle, and
fear that permeates the majority of situations. Our inability or unwill-
ingness to communicate in healthy ways creates much conflict. People
of all cultures are economically, ecologically, politically, and spiritually
estranged from one another. The insidious "social" cancers and the
global disregard for justice have created a rift between all humans, re-
sulting in epidemic violence, unemployment, poverty, hunger, drug
abuse, and racial conflict throughout the world.

In our most quiet, reflective moments, we probably realize that this
dismal situation need not be. Most reasonable people agree that we
can, and deserve to, experience world order, as overwhelming a thought
as this may be. Rather than begin to change the world, perhaps we may
need to be less ambitious, and act on the local, individual, and personal levels.

Let us contemplate the possible uses and applications of the Tao
mentoring model and imagine its impact on families, education, business management, political negotiations, and other relationships with
people in all arenas of life. At its core, the Chinese philosophy of Taoism exhibits passion for the interdependence and harmony of all
systems and that each of us depends on the well-being of the whole.
The philosophy encourages humble visions of a healthy, harmonious
world, "Tashun," the Great Harmony. The golden age of China, when
the great Tao prevailed, is referred to as the period of Tat'ung, the period of the Great Commonwealth. It was a time of universal harmony,
peace, cooperation, and respect for one another. Tat'ung was the Confucian utopia of attainable social order and moral perfection.

The creation of such a perfect social order is probably beyond our
capability and power. However, it is reasonable to expect that on an individual basis we can reduce the world's problems to a level much
lower than that which we presently endure. Confucius believed in
small beginnings and a gradual expansion of vision. He emphasized
the cultivation of self as a first step and creating harmony within the
immediate family before considering the community . . . the country
. . . the world. To try to begin on a more grandiose scale would be like

sowing seeds without weeding the garden. We must not interfere with our capability of influencing others in a positive way. How can we step aside so that our influence can shine through to others without placing them in total eclipse?

Tao mentoring is offered as a humble, simple beginning to help all of us to "get out of the way" of ourselves and one another. We, Chungliang and Jerry, know from our cooperative collaboration and partnership how fortunate we are to experience the effect of Tao mentoring within our relationship and our personal lives. We are most grateful and humble for this fortune of mutual giving and receiving. This experience has opened up our eyes to possibilities for global change. We don't presume to have the answer to any of the world's problems; we are simply excited about what we've experienced with Tao mentoring on a microscale and wonder, "What if . . . ?" For ourselves, we are enjoying our "Tui Shou Dance" together as we watch each other bloom, expand, and come of age in our writing and all other aspects of our personal lives. We notice in our immediate networks how this dynamic, humanistic way of interrelating affects others. We mentor others, and they are now turning around and mentoring us with mutual respect and caring.

Global considerations possibly need to take into account the "ripple effect" phenomenon that Confucius talked about. The Tao reminds us of how a small pebble, when dropped in water, causes endless numbers of concentric circles to ripple outward, touching everything in their wake. How we relate to ourselves is how we relate to others. By cultivating the powerful "self," we begin to offer the possibility of change to those in our world; change comes from the individual heart and fans outward, creating a unified, interconnected community. The key is to go beyond self-indulgence and reach out to others close to us, creating harmony even with those who are different, those we don't even understand, and then begin to see how, in our differentness, we are all linked.

Imagine life as one big circular dance in which all beings and things are interdependent. What if everyone were aligned with the basic law of reciprocity, where the intent is to give, to help, and in return receive one hundredfold for all our efforts? What if the emphasis were on quality rather than quantity? Process rather than product? How would this shift affect our educational, political, and ecological systems?

What if leaders of the world used a Tao mentoring approach to resolve international conflict? Imagine them being nonjudgmental, humble, and kind, leaders who seek our intuitive reactions to problematic situations and encourage positive focus through modeling. How could we use the Tao to accomplish our goals of balancing the ecosystem and protecting our rain forests? Visualize classrooms filled with mentor-educators who experienced Tao mentoring in their teacher training. What would it be like to be an athlete coached by a Tao mentor? Imagine summit meetings and conferences being conducted within the boundaries of this new paradigm. What would our work environments be like if managers and employees related to one another in this new way? If greed could be replaced by a concern for wildlife, imagine the implications of Tao mentoring for endangered species. Consider societies where the elderly are looked to as wise, valuable teachers and citizens rather than valued only for how much they contribute to the economy. Imagine if education were viewed as a process, as something with intrinsic value rather than as a means to better salaries and lifestyles. Visualize a world where countries and organizations are flexible and adaptable, finding spiritual avenues to resolve difficulties; where cooperation and partnership are honored with high regard for human dignity. What changes would occur if we began thinking that we belong to our environment rather than own it? Imagine blossoming to our full human potential in a setting of unconditional nurturance.

Harmony and balance are the natural order for all things. All systems throughout the world coexist in an interdependent network. With this in mind, imagine what it would be like to act in alignment with what is natural, with what's supposed to be, rather than to force its opposite.

Let Tao mentoring encourage us to notice our natural interdependent relationships with the world and how we coexist in a harmonious network of people capable of creating a greater whole, together rather than separate.

Jerry Lynch
Center for Tao Mentoring and Performance
2100 W. Drake Road, Suite 276
Fort Collins, Colorado 80526

C. L. Al Huang
Living Tao Foundation
P.O. Box 846
Urbana, Illinois 61801